All About Me

People I Know

By Meg Gaertner

level 1 little blue readers

www.littlebluehousebooks.com

Little Blue House is distributed by North Star Editions:
sales@northstareditions.com | 888-417-0195

Produced for Little Blue House by Red Line Editorial.

Photographs ©: Wavebreakmedia/iStockphoto, cover; FatCamera/iStockphoto, 4; kali9/iStockphoto, 7; bowdenimages/iStockphoto, 8–9; Marius Pirvu/Shutterstock Images, 11; JohnnyGreig/iStockphoto, 12–13, 16 (top left); Steve Debenport/iStockphoto, 15; DragonImages/iStockphoto, 16 (bottom left); LightField Studios/Shutterstock Images, 16 (top right); skynesher/iStockphoto, 16 (bottom right)

Library of Congress Control Number: 2019908250

ISBN
978-1-64619-002-7 (hardcover)
978-1-64619-041-6 (paperback)
978-1-64619-080-5 (ebook pdf)
978-1-64619-119-2 (hosted ebook)

Printed in the United States of America
Mankato, MN
012020

About the Author

Meg Gaertner enjoys reading, writing, dancing, and being outside. She lives in Minnesota.

Table of Contents

teacher

People I Know

I know a teacher.
She teaches me
new things.

I know a librarian.

He helps me find books.

I love to read them.

librarian

I know a dentist.

He cleans my teeth.

dentist

I know a mail carrier.

He comes to my house.

He brings me a package.

mail carrier
package

I know a doctor.
She helps me
stay healthy.

doctor

I know a police officer.

He keeps me safe.

Glossary

doctor

police officer

mail carrier

teacher

Index